Rudra

Rudra

ABIRAMI P. KURUKKAL

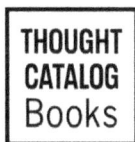

THOUGHT CATALOG Books

BROOKLYN, NY

**THOUGHT
CATALOG
Books**

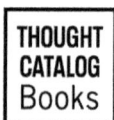

Hand lettering by GloriAnne Rose Dairo. Cover photo by Joel Filipe/Unsplash.

Published by Thought Catalog Books, a publishing house owned by The Thought & Expression Co., Williamsburg, Brooklyn.

First edition, 2018

ISBN: 978-1945796746

Printed and bound in the United States.

10 9 8 7 6 5 4 3 2 1

this one is for you, Mom

you are the woman who showed me
how to live in all levels of hellfire
and still come out of it all
unscathed

the meaning of Rudra

Rudra is a Sanskrit word that is mainly associated with a Rigvedic deity, the Lord of Storms. Translated, the word Rudra means "the one who roars, the mightiest one." The word also has many meanings that can vary according to the poetic application and individual interpretation, but in short, it refers to the personification of power, both glorious and frightening. The word is also used in direct reference to Lord Shiva, one of the principle deities of Hinduism and the God of destruction/rebirth.

foreword

My first book, *Remember Me as a Time of Day*, was self-published through Amazon in 2016 and is a collection of essays and poetry about grief and loss. It is a raw and unfiltered tribute to my late father who passed away in 2013. The book is a collection of both essays and poetry which depicts the emotion and the journey behind living on after the death of a loved one. It is my story of grief, depression, denial, and finding the strength not to give up on a life without my father.

Rudra is my second book, and this book will be different. Published by my good friends at Thought Catalog, the theme of this book revolves around taking back the power that gets lost when a person goes through a period of trauma, emptiness, and lack of purpose in their lives. It tackles two opposing forces: self-love and self-loathing. The poetry explores the eventual destruction of the latter and the rebirth of the former. In the last four years since my father's death, I have felt, on many occasions, empty and deserted. I have felt abandoned and unloved. I have felt my faith slip away from me and almost disappear. **Rudra is about taking back that loss of self and reigniting the fire that was put out by the fear of rejection.**

In essence, *Rudra* is about the destruction of self-hate and stigma. It is about resurrecting ourselves from the chains of self-doubt and freeing our voices from eternal silence. It is a manifestation of courage. The poems explore the depth of the importance of self-care and discuss the rebirth of resilience, a mission to rescue souls almost drowning in their rivers of desperation, anxiety, pain, and trauma.

This book hopes to serve as a reminder that we are not here to be repressed.

We are here to roar.

dear reader

there is no contents page.

the poems in this book are scattered
like stars on a summer night.
there is no real order in life,
and we do not always live according to our plans.
that is why the compilation of this book is dedicated to
individual discovery.
there are poems of destruction, sadness, despair, and death.
there are poems of love, rebirth, kindness, and empowerment.
there are long poems, and there are brief thoughts.
they are all breathing in harmony together,
nestled in no particular order,
amongst the pages of this book.

may your heart find the depthless peace that it seeks.
may you encounter lasting comfort,
power, and
reassurance in these pages.

introduction

Do not write for an audience. Do not seek to be applauded or discovered or celebrated. Write for the sheer joy of having taken your heart and shaved slices of it off into thoughts that floated down as words that took firm hold onto paper as poetry.

Write for the lost souls who live a hundred thousand miles away and decide to live another day because something you wrote, a word or a sentence, sparked a sudden warmth of hope inside their empty hearts so strongly that they decided to hide the rope, the knives, and the pills.

Write for the generations that are to come, so that when one of them decides to search for the meaning of the historic Internet in their advanced times, they may find your work and remember how to live through love and friendship, not digitalised falsehood.

Write for the present. Write for the girl who sits alone at lunch and the boy who tried but failed to stand up to the popular kid at school who keeps giving him bruises like weekly Sunday brunch.

Write so that you inspire change. Write so that you initiate the birth of kindness in the heartbeat of others so that they create endless ripples that will one day save the world.

Write, so that you have done your best to manifest positivity and joy into the universe. Write for the world. Our world.

Write in all your different colours, textures, and hues. Write without fear.

Write your truth.

—they asked me what I would say to a young writer

I feel sorry for the sun

Why?

Because the moon always has stars to keep her company
but the sun is so bright
that she keeps scaring off the clouds.
It must be very lonely.
Maybe that's the price
for being full of such powerful light.

you're always in love with the things that will kill you
this is why you write songs
this is why you write your poetry
that bleeds metaphors and melancholy
you hope that if you turn your heart
into forms of art
then maybe all those things
that are killing you
will kill you slower

—on drugs of the heart

and that's the thing about wanting things you can't have
there is no silver lining
sometimes, the silver lining is the suffering
and it still somehow feels like heaven
even when the silence feels like
a sword in your heart
love drowns you
and you would rather be pulled down
by its icy waters
than suffocate on the surface

—on lonely love

I paint my nails when I am sad. It's a subconscious act, something that I no longer think about, just do. There are several things I do when the hurt swells up and I need my hands to get busy, to distract my mind from the heaviness that accumulates in my heart. I pick up a black marker and write poetry that turns into essays that turn into sagas. I tie up my hair into a ball at the top of my head and untie it again in a cycle that continues every half hour. I wash my face and I walk around the house, not really following my legs or my thought process either, just pretending to be a wanderer in this closed space. I listen to indie music. I listen to the silence. I listen to my own heartbeat and count every motion, every throb, every tear. I kiss my mother on the cheek and I make my bed for the fifth time.

I paint my nails when I am sad. Sometimes maroon. *Mostly black.*

some things
we endure quietly
almost silently

some things
we endure like a beast
unleashed,
after centuries
of captivity

the roar is so loud
that thunder
seems like
a whisper

kindness is golden
kindness is magic
kindness will pave
the way
for a better world
kindness will eradicate
all evil
if only we let it
if only we use it

                              —we already have our cure

my heart is a cemetery
of a thousand *almosts*

it almost gave up
it almost let go
it almost drowned
it almost died

yet still, it beats
yet still, it survived

—this heart is steel

I don't know how to do anything in pieces. I come into people's lives like a hurricane. I uproot their ideas of love and fill their voids with floods of my presence and passion. I will never disrupt your day against your will, but once given entry, I do not make an exit without leaving my mark. Sometimes, there are casualties.

Sometimes, they make one out of me.

Small talk is a mission. You want to tell the person how you still miss your dad, so much so that you still sometimes wake up shivering from a dream where he was smiling, so close but still out of your reach. You want to tell the person how most of your money gets spent on food and that your idea of therapy is walking around in a stationery shop because the silent presence of books and moleskin journals and paintbrushes has the power to comfort you after a long and miserable day. You want to tell them how you love long phone calls and that effort means everything to you and that you suck at goodbyes, that's why it means the world to you when someone says the first hello, calls first, texts first without being told. You want late night conversations and you want to tell them you're an old-school romantic with a battered heart and the tendency to simply start crying without warning, sometimes because you are sad but most times because you are unable to contain the flood of emotion that fills you every time you are happy, angry, or afraid. You want to tell them all this, you really do. You want to be honest and open and vulnerable hold nothing back. You want to talk about all the things you managed to survive and all the love you're capable of. You want all that but you remember you're not there yet. Before all that comes the small talk.

But how do you tell them you weren't built for small talk?

Sitting in coffee shops alone has become one of my favourite things to do lately. I find a sense of calm when I sit there, alone but not alone, invisible and entirely unseen. Home? I have not known what a home is for a very long time. My lungs are torn from running without a moment to stop and breathe. My heart has roamed for years in search of warmth, and sometimes it resigns likes this in the corners of a café where the steam of an espresso or the foam of a mocha frappé is comforting, even if only momentarily. I am silent but my mind is shouting. I wonder what the couple in the corner is talking about; they're holding hands but their eyes are diverted and empty. I wonder if the barista has a child at home who's waiting for her to come home and cook dinner. I wonder if love is fiction and all these stories that have happy endings are only true until the part where there's a happy ending. Maybe the boat did sink, the marriage did end, the train had already gone. Maybe authors just added a happy ending to give us hope, to mask the bitter truth, like a child looking up at a rainbow in a black sky. Like a tablespoon of sugar in black coffee.

Like the sickly-sweet finality of honey-coated goodbyes.

The earth does not die when you fall flat on your face from tripping over a stone by mistake. The earth does not condemn you for taking up space when all your peers have settled down yet you're still stuck in a mundane life unchanged. Your miracle still on its way, just a little late. The earth does not spit on you with distaste when you fail to be perfect or when you forget an important date. The soil does not burn to ash when your heart breaks open and you lose all your broken patches of desperately collected faith.

The earth forgives and flowers bloom again.

The earth may go dry after a drought but it comes back to life after the rain. The earth does not dwell forever in decay and dust and dormant pain. It embraces its children with love and grace—including you—and your life is certainly not in vain. This bitterness you feel is a burden, I know, but bury it, my dear. Bury it and vow to begin all over again. Bury all this heartache. Bury all this self-hate.

—you forgot to love yourself, didn't you?

and though they tried
to crack you open
here you are, still whole
and though they tried
to break your courage
here you are, still brave
and though they tried
to bury you alive
here you are, still standing

and though they tried
to kill your spirit
here you are, still breathing

you wanted so badly
to be the fire
you wanted to be
a light so bright
yet you forgot
how much it can burn

sitting in a boat
in the middle of the sea
oars taken away
from me
and I've been using
my hands
trying to paddle
to dry land, but
I'm losing the
strength
to carry on
all I see are stretches
of ocean and
the setting suns

—what depression feels like

some days
I am the
OCEAN
some days
I wish I
had DROWNED
in it.

you shouldn't have
to grip love
with iron hands
trying your hardest
to make sure that
it doesn't flee

real love
does not treat you
like an enemy
it does not try
to leave

it brings you home
it sets you free

time is slow, like a snail
lingering like a shadow
an echo
a hole
you have essays
in your voice
but a deep silence
in your soul
you wander around
while dragging parts of you
that got chipped away
with the years
you don't recognise
yourself anymore

you miss being whole

you don't need someone
who treats your love
like it's simply
a leisure activity

you need someone
who treats your heart
like it's their home
like it's their only identity

—on the love you deserve

it takes *courage* to be kind

violence and cruelty are the
children of *cowardice*

when people look at me and say
you look exactly like your father
I feel divided between ecstasy
and devastation
delighted to be his clone
but painfully aware that
it's not the same thing as
having him around

it's like having a photograph
of a rose
you can look at it for
as long as you like
but you will never be able
to hold it
feel its texture
get pricked by its thorns
be comforted by its petals
smell its fine fragrance
water it, cherish it
or protect it

all you can do is stare
eyes raw with a hunger
that never dies

don't get me wrong
she wants to know you
she wants to give you her time
she wants to give you a chance
to take up a role in her life
but she is afraid
she is tired
she is wary
she is playing it safe

and why wouldn't she?

the last time she cared
too much
he crushed her heart
with his careless games
the last time she trusted
someone, enough
to let him inside her home
he set the whole place
up in flames

—reasons why she holds back

they play
with your heart
and expect you
to be grateful for it

as if the pain they gave you was paradise

trust me when I say that
I don't need you to define me
I have survived loss repeatedly
I have woken up to witness my life
being wrenched out of my hands
and I have started a fresh new page
over and over again
I have taken darkness and wrapped it
around me like a blanket to keep me
warm and safe amidst the wars
raging on around me
I have fallen prey to wolves, and
then risen out of the bloodshed
the pack purring like kittens
at my feet
I have been so afraid that I have
reached a point where fear has become
my friend, an ally, a familiar tingle
a tickle, no longer a foe
I do not need your presence
nor your pity
I am the northern star, the winter winds
the sunset on the southern shores
I am the only solace that I need

I am free

you shoot words, laced
with hate
like poisonous arrows
at my back
you threaten me with your
bold voice and your
war dances

tell me,
would you still speak
if I turned to face you?
would you still
be brave
if this cage was opened?

to every person who
has ever broken
pieces off
my heart

thank you

it is because of you
that I now know
what I do not want
from another
human

it is because of you
that I now choose
to be kinder
to other
humans

you love them
even when they leave you
and you trust them
even when they deceive you

—reasons why you feel so empty

I do not let these walls
come down so easily
and even when
it seems that
I have
there are mountains left
uncovered in me
there are secrets left
as deep as the sea

I cry in locked cubicles of empty malls

It's not that the malls are empty. Most times, they are packed with the sounds of children screaming, heels clicking, and a hundred voices all blended into a buzzing bustling symphony that is not in the least relaxing. But I don't mind because I don't want it to be relaxing. I want it to be distracting, a camouflage to my chaos, the voices drowning out the sound of my sobs. I want to be unheard. I want to be invisible. I want to sit on the stone-cold floor on my bag, my legs crossed, my heart leaking drops of pain that I want nobody to see. I want the sounds of the taps and the dryer and the radio overhead to guard me from exposure at my cubicle door so that I can shed this skin of self-loathing without an audience, without a scene. No, the mall is loud and there's laughter and there are really bright lights and trying to lure shoppers into shops and there are a lot of different sounds and stories and sales where stuff is 70% off, but that's not the point. That's why I take these quick bathroom breaks during my lunch hour because these plain sounds bring sweet silence.

And the silence is the only thing that soothes my sadness.

you destroy people
there, I said it
you destroy people, as if
they are made of clay
as if they are games to played
as if they are slaves

but when did you forget
that it was those shoulders
that held your weight
it was those fists
that you bit into
when you were in pain?

you say they are peasants
you say their poverty
makes you want to gag
no, my dear
don't you see?
they are the real royalty
and your ungrateful heart
is not even on par
with their rags

here you stand
your axe in hand
you chop at my arms
you chop at my chest
you chop at my skin
all I hear is
chop
chop
chop
all I feel is
nothing
you tried to tear me
into pieces
but you could never touch
my soul within

—*keep cutting*

her freckles were stars
her dark spots
were black moons

her heart was the treasure
her every move
your muse

I'll be an endless sea of forgiveness
when you need redemption
but
I will also drown you in my depths
like a corpse, if you ever try
to corrupt my waters

she's an ocean of kindness
a home for many kinds of aquatic wildlife
her waters the living area for
dependant souls
yet, she is so lonely
that she is willing to crash her waves
onto jagged rocks, just to feel something
she is willing to let her purity
be fouled by leaked oils and dumped plastic
just to feel like she is alive, like she
is breathing, moving
she is willing to battle storms
and drown sailors in broken ships
just to know some company
she is not evil
she does not mean to hurt or destroy
but somehow, she ends up
sinking just about anything
that gets too close
she ends up engulfing anything
that can't swim in her waves
even though her intention
was to only *embrace*

I have been swimming in deep self-loathing
and self-doubt for so long that
I know what it feels like
to just want it all to
just be over, to
just end.

I don't know much, but I know all about grief.

That is why I
always try my hardest
to reach into the waters and
save as many sinking souls as I can,
because nobody saved me. I had to save myself.

girl, you are too kind
all the damn time
and that's a problem
don't you know?
this world does not handle
gentle things well
haven't you seen
enough horror movies
oops, sorry, I meant romantic comedies
to realise that the comedy
the biggest joke
is the one that cared
a little too often
a little too much
you're a crutch, a toy
yet girl, here you are
you keep slipping on ice
and blaming the sun
but isn't it always you
that's always on the run?
breaking your neck for people
who see you as a tissue to
blow snot out their noses,
a joker, a jolly good "friend"
just a little bit of harm(less) fun?

the reason why I feel like
I am better off alone
is that I can never do things
simply
or moderately
or casually

my love is always large
and loud
and I lay down
my life
for those whom I love

it is because of this
that people let go
of me
it is because of this
that they say I'm
a liability

It's November and here you are, beating yourself black and blue for letting eleven months slip by and not yet having accomplished everything. Here you are, saying hurtful things to your reflection in the mirror, blaming yourself for the declining bank balance, unpaid bills and the bitterness. You would say you're the reason that the weather is so unpleasant, too, if you could. It's almost the end of the year. December is here, and you are back to old self-blame game that you're so good at. Back to the wild and anxious thoughts that you had struggled so badly to tame, which you have once again let loose. Yet, you forget that you are still here, still standing. Still spreading kindness that you just can't seem to offer yourself. Here you are, alive after conflicts that should have killed you, *but only made you stronger.* Here you are, a rock and a source of comfort and courage to those who are lucky enough to earn your love. Look at you, *look at you.* Not your flaws, not your mistakes, not your regrets, not the ghosts of your past.

Look at *you.* You are a star walking on the earth's surface and *you still think you are insignificant.*

Because sometimes the people we love cannot love us back. The places we want to go are not within our reach. The past is a burden that cannot be put down. It weighs down on us and that weight is a constant reminder of what it feels like to house an empty heart. Sometimes you end up looking back, and the years that slipped by don't make any sense. Sometimes being alone is the only thing that brings peace of any kind.

You want answers. You want to look into your memories but you stop as soon as you start, afraid of what you'll find.

I have never loved with doubt.
my love screams like
a woman giving birth—
willing and wanted and focused lovingly
on the pain she has chosen.
my love is footprints in concrete—you cannot erase away
the memories of me with water.
you cannot exorcise me away,
no matter the number of roosters
you slaughter.

there are *stories*
in ME that are
yet to be TOLD

stories of
SURVIVAL
stories of
gold

I run from me grief sometimes.
actually, in reality I sprint
tripping over my ten toes
like they were made of rubber
instead of flesh and bone

I run at 1000 miles an hour
trying to forget the icy pain
that loss leaves inside you
the hollow vault can be filled
with smoke for a little while
but eventually, the silence
will start echoing again
and then, what then?

that question terrifies me
I'll get through today
and maybe the next day too
but what then?
what if there will be a day
that I can't survive through?
what if everything gets too much?
who do I run to?

—I wish I could say you, Dad

I am not a monster, though I may seem like one for cutting people off in the cold way that I do. I used to be the girl who would be on the floor, begging people to stay. *Don't leave me!* I would scream. *Don't let me go. I'll do anything! I'm sorry. I'm sorry. I'm sorry.*

But I'm on my feet now. I'm not sorry anymore.

I have been that girl who would let you back in, break down the door for you if I had to, even when God was telling me to turn the lock and throw away the key. I was that girl who just couldn't say no because for some reason, the word *no* was a poison on my tongue that I could not swallow, and I was not the kind to commit suicide, so I said *yes*. I didn't know then that *yes* meant losing the brakes to my car and failing my driver's test. I didn't know that *yes* meant saying *yes* to self-immolation, *yes* meant the death of self-respect.

I am not a monster, even though at times I may seem like one for walking away without looking back, despite your desperate calls. I used to be that girl who would turn right back around and welcome you with open arms.

But I've got wings now. *I don't walk backwards anymore.*

they don't want the crazy ones.
no, they only want the crazy ones for sweet conversations.
they only want the rare and artistic ones as a distraction,
a temporary solution.

but they don't want the girls with big hearts
and loud souls to stick around
too long.

they want us like bandages
but never forever by their side.
never as the bride.

love will kill you
repeat after me
love will kill you
but bear in mind that
it will be a sweet death
darkness dipped in
maple syrup
horrors coated with icing
and powdered sugar

love will have
your hearse booked
way before you've
met his eyes
love will have
your heart buried
way before you actually die
love will make you
confess your truth
and declare that
it is all a lie

—the dark side of love

you can try your best
to mould a sculpture from stone
but some people are stones that
do not want to be touched

some people are solid
and unwavering
and cannot be moved
you can chip away at their edges
but you will not find
a silver lining

you can try to make them into art
but you will be left with nothing
but a pile of dust

you deserve to be loved with
endless passion
you deserve the kind of love
that fills your heart,
then overflows

you remind me
of rose petals
on fire

something beautiful
that is plagued
by pain

—let me be your rain

kindness is not permission
to inflict pain
kindness does not mean
I surrender

she is a strong woman

she is talented
at muffling her screams
at polishing her surface
at covering her scars

this is why everyone thinks that
nothing can break her

I am unable to understand this thing we call a spark. There is no such thing. There is only the inferno that unconsciously ignites every time we find someone that seems to just stop our heart from beating. Their affection is blinding like the sun, and it binds our senses into a knot. We are unaware that we are burning, so we call it a spark.

We think we're sleeping when we're drowning,
so we never see the sharks.

I have not always been
deserving of compassion
I have not always been
understanding of human nature

this is why I do not hate
the people who forget
to practice kindness with me
but that does not mean
I can be taken for a fool

my affection is never
an invitation for attack
don't enter my heart like
acid through a crack

it is a courageous thing
to be vulnerable
to open your heart and
to let that pain flow

don't ever let anyone
make you feel weak
for doing so

promise yourself
that from this day forward
you will abandon the
destructive habit
of reaching inside yourself
to pull out your heart
from its safe abode
only to put it
in the hands of people
who don't value
your kindness, until
your heart is deflated
your patience is dead
and your soul is drowning
plagued with the blues
promise me that you
will learn how to
love yourself
too

—stop breaking your own heart

It's a large ensemble of emotions that are an inch from the edge of toppling over themselves. One minute, every little thing brings immeasurable joy and you're excited to be alive. Then the next minute, the world is your enemy and your room is your biggest comfort, your most reliable refuge. Kindness from strangers makes you cry because you have never known what it feels like to have a solid place to call home. You love road trips and French fries and singing along to Ed Sheeran songs in the car, but you don't have the energy to do all that and be left all alone all over again because saying goodbye has become your trend. You are happy and hollow at the same time. You promise your heart that this is the last time that you will ever care too much about anyone, but then it is left bleeding out on the pavement, as usual, and you're back to trying to figure out if it will ever mend.

—I am still trying to find the good in goodbye

we worship things
that drip with poison
deluded into believing
they are pure

I could say I am angry
that you're not here
but I would be lying
because one of the two
is not true

yes, I am mad
that you're gone
but I won't say that
you're absent, because
you never left

you're always alive
in my mind
like a solid prayer
like a tumour I never
want to cure

like unpaid debt
that I never want to pay off
you're the rainbow that
I wish I could tattoo onto
the sky

I won't say hello
when you visit me
in my dreams
because I never
said goodbye

—another poem on grief

I want to say that forgiving is easy, but it is not. Forgiving someone who strangled your self-esteem and pricked your mind with razors labelled with *narcissism* but mistaken for compassion is like hearing a siren that's loud and red and just doesn't stop ringing. You wish you didn't have to listen to it.

But you are injured,
and every crime scene needs an ambulance.

you want to take things back
take it all back
if you could

you want to go back it time
and place duct tape over
your mouth
to shut yourself up
from saying things
that will crack
the perfectly smooth surface
of your life

but you know that
you can't
because in that moment
you meant every word
and you regret it now
that you did

—I'm sorry I meant what I said

you've never cooked before
but lately, you've been seen
in the kitchen a lot more
you search a new pasta recipe
you learn how to make white sauce
even if it's from a
mix hot water and stir
sachet
you pick out spices and
you learn how to use them
you cook because it gives you
an escape, a release
and when you buy your list
of ingredients
it gives you something to
look forward to
other than the ceiling of
your room or
the screen of your phone
you cook because it allows you
to create something, even if
it's not perfect, and in the process
your heart and your mind
are busy concentrating
let simmer for five more minutes
as you follow instructions
that silence, the loud yearning
in your soul

—when depression is on the menu

the moon is smaller than
the sun
but it does not mean
it lacks beauty

you give away your blood and bones
trying to find affection, adoration
and acceptance
you'd trade your soul for it
if you could
you don't want riches and gold
just a hand to hold
you don't ask for much
just a kind word
just a phone call
just a voice at the other end
of the line, saying things like
I'm thinking of you
and
I'm here for you, okay?
just the warm feeling of
being cared for,
being needed
being important to someone
a sliver of a chance that
someone thinks that
you are worth their time
that you are worth loving

if you are a man
and you decide that
it is okay to
not speak up when
your boss makes
a sexist joke in a meeting
or when men in the street
catcall a woman walking home
or when they think it's
absolutely fine to report
woman claims assault
instead of
woman assaulted
when talking about abuse in
the media
then you, sir
are choosing to overlook
the problem.

you are choosing to promote
the problem by ignoring it
you are choosing to keep
your capacity to save millions
inactive and dormant
instead of using it
to become our allies

your silence means you are choosing
to sit on the fence, hence
you have decided
to become one with the oppression

I am an ocean that has
somehow started to believe
that it is a raindrop
so, when people tell me
that I am insignificant,
I almost started to believe them

but the ocean can never
be small, subtle
or insignificant
the ocean can never cease to matter
no matter how loudly
the grey clouds chatter

I'm messy.

I love the colour black, but I also adore splashes of colour here and there. I say I hate summer, but my hands always yearn for warmth in the middle of storms, in the heart of winter. I crave affection, but sprint when anyone tries to approach me with their kindness. I prefer my books stacked orderly while the rest of my room suffers in disorderly doom. I sing when I'm sad and I dream with my eyes open.

I'm a mess, yes. *But beautiful things are sometimes broken.*

the good that you do
it will find you
and it will save you
in your darkest hour

you treat dragons, as if
they are doves
but kindness is not
in their nature, my dear
fire demands
a certain element of fear

they said I am *emotional*
like it's a bad thing
yes, I am overpowered by
my feelings all the time
I don't listen to my mind
because I am too busy
serving as a slave
to my heart
so, when you say that
I am too emotional
if you mean that I am
too compassionate
too empathetic
too passionate
too strong
too courageous
too fierce
when it comes to
defending *what's right*
celebrating *what's good*
and opposing the oppression
then yes
I am emotional
and I am blessed to be
this way

—*empowered (not enslaved) by emotions*

I do not need your *it will be okay*
I do not need your *it will get better*
I do not need your *it will change*

I need your *everything is shitty, but I'm staying*
I need your *everything is broken, but I'm still solid*
I need your *everything sucks, but you have me*

There is no recovery when it comes to grief. There is only growth, and growth does not always mean it will be easy or smooth. Growth is painful, moving on is painful, and the grief is always growing with you. You can feel the years pushing past you like a bustling crowd that doesn't stop to take note of whether you were trampled. There is no bright green neon exit sign that will help you escape, because reality is a stage and you are the final act that everyone is waiting for. It's always you. The bearer of responsibility. The giver of reassurances. The reliever of burdens. The constant chew toy. The strongest oak in the forest. Your branches are sagging with the weight of everything and everyone.

Your heart is crying because of the *overcrowding*.

There is always that lingering apprehension. Eyes sharp as a razor, looking out for the chain to break. The ship to sink. Your lungs have been full to the brim with so much water that air has now become the enemy. Your heart has been at sea for so long that drowning feels like floating and dry land just seems like foreign territory. You don't expect the light to find you. You don't expect life to be kind to you anymore. Every little knock on the door is as loud as a bullet. Every brief smile from a stranger looks like a leer. Every grey cloud seems magnified to your eyes and you start to fear storms that are not yet born. You try so hard to see the rainbow that everyone keeps pointing out to you, but the rain keeps falling like drops of ice on your soul. There is silence and then there is chaos. The world seems like a big empty park where all the swing sets are rusty and all the joggers moody. You sit alone at a bench, your hair messy and your clothes drenched. You want it all to end, but somehow you manage to get out of bed the next day and it starts all over again.

—what it feels like to live with anxiety

It's a lonely road some days, and you want nothing more than to park your life in the shade of something stable. Reliable. Permanent. Normal. Oh, how you crave normalcy. How you wish you had a plain and simple life where you have a childhood home, old friends, a hometown you grew up in and people who you've known all your days. Instead, you're a foreigner in your birthplace, a commoner in a land across the sea and an oddity, no matter what colour the flag may be. Your eyes are a haven for many who seek healing, but you have never known a place called home, a place to rest your brittle bones. You are a traveller, and this lifetime is made up of many lifetimes all squeezed into replays of trauma and festivals and celebrations and tragedy. You've lost count of your many sorrows and many blessings. *You no longer regret being gifted with all this chaos.*

You've taken it all to heart, and so, it's proved to be fuel for your art.

electric colour spilled
on black

energy
in everything

　　　　　　　—they asked me to describe myself

these salty tears
are stinging my cheeks
like hot acid burning
through skin

these sudden fears
are pricking my heart
with holes, revealing
the emptiness within

—anxiety

"those who love you will never leave you"

ah, but what if leaving
was the only way
to prove
their love?

what if letting go
was the only way
to let you
live?

to save you?

—*the other side of the story*

you laugh
like crystals chiming
in the wind
when all your body wants
is to lay down
in the arms of
the warm earth
and sob itself
to sleep

—sad days teach strength

you cannot
BREAK her
and then expect
her to SING
like you did not
just DRINK her BLOOD
and rip out
her wings

you can either be the lightning
that strikes down someone's life
or you can be the light
that destroys their darkness

—decide

Some days, there's no feeling. No darkness to haunt you and no light to help you. Some days, it's nothing but numbness. You sit and stare at the wall, and when you get tired of that, you lay and stare at the ceiling. There is no deep sorrow or confusion. There are no tears staining the pillow. There are no weak moments or sudden rays of hope shining through your soul. There are no broken hearts or breakdowns on the bathroom floor. There is no sudden moment of clarity or raging fury. There is nothing out of the ordinary. Nothing emotional. Nothing crazy or noteworthy of talk. There are no visits to the emergency room or tearful phone calls to a friend at 3 AM in the early hours of the morning after a meltdown.

Some days there is nothing left but numbness. *Stillness*.

I tend to forget
that self-love is not conceit
that self-pity is not a comfort
that self-respect is not a crime

I tend to forget
that taking a day, a week, a month off
to clear my head of pain
is not a waste of time

—a reminder that self-care is vital

you think you see moisture
but I'm an ocean
that has merely chosen
to be standing still

you think you see a flicker
but I'm a wildfire
that has merely decided
not to kill

if it leaves you
do not cling

do not listen
to the pain that it sings

you are destined
for far better things

—*open the door for what wants to leave*

in your moment of misery
a friend does not waver
a friend does not abandon

one who does
is not a friend
nor deserves your friendship

on some days
my soul is tired
its glow is dim

I am learning to accept
that this, too, is okay

fire will burn flesh
whether you are
king
or slave

your gold may matter while
you breathe
but when you die
everything returns to the soil

how do you intend
to patch up
your purple heart
and stitch its ripped seams
if you refuse
to let go
of all the things
that make your wounds bleed?

—drop your weapons, darling

life is meant to shake you
it is meant to bring you
to your knees
that is how you break out
of your cocoon
that is how you realise
you were destined
to have wings
from the very beginning

if she loves you
do not take that for granted

do not treat her like a ghost
and then wonder why she's gone

my tears don't always cleanse me
nor heal me

some days, they make me sink
and I let them drown me

letting go sometimes becomes
the cure

letting go saved me
and brought me back to the surface

I am a person who harbours
cavernous sadness
inside me

I possess a caged heart that
yearns to be set free
to breathe

                    —*they asked me to say something painfully honest*

I am not the cheap nail polish
on your broken nails
that you can bite your teeth into
or wipe away with cotton wool
whenever you favour acetone
more than you'll ever favour
a real conversation

I am the skin beneath the nail
delicate, but strong and solid
I am real and raw and not
easily reached, even if you
manage to scrape away the nail
to touch me, I still guarantee
that you will be screaming

why is it that
we always nourish the things
that destroy us
and starve the things
that could have been our salvation?

Nobody knows what it feels like to have your lungs full of water until you're trying to reach up out of the deep end for a gulp of air. Is it so hard to be kind and loving and supportive and protective of the people who struggle a little bit more than usual with this thing called waking up in the morning and this other thing called getting through each day? Why does it take dozens of centuries of tragedy and TV shows like "13 Reasons Why" for us to realise that depression and peer pressure and pain are not jokes? Why is it that we perceive this reality as a wisp of smoke, as a dizzy silly daydream?

Why do we overlook and ignore signs of upcoming storms and cries for help, *no matter how loudly they scream?*

—let's end the stigma. let's save lives.

disappointments
can teach you courage
because every time
you are let down
you realise that
you can always decide
to stand back up
if you want to
and that takes courage

that takes strength

maybe she doesn't respond
to your needs anymore
because she is tired of being
answered with silence

maybe she doesn't react to
your pain anymore, because
you never did anything to stop
her wounds from bleeding

maybe all you were was the
highest form of violence
maybe all she knew was
the purest form of healing

maybe that is why she is leaving

how does hurting the innocent
heal your wounds?
how does shedding the blood
of a bystander
fix the leaks in your heart?
how does organising
the end of someone
who has not even touched
a hair on the top of
your head
give you a brand new start?

—on senseless violence

I write like
ink
is the MEDICINE
and PAPER is the
cure

wait for the one
who will hurt you
but only because
the happiness is so great
that your heart
can't hold it in anymore
so joyful that
your heartstrings stretch
uncomfortably

I have reached a stage in my life where I do not expect anything to be linear anymore. I accept the storms that rage and the calm that follows without question. I do not stop the shadows that follow me around. I do not confront the fears that are instilled in my heart on cold days. I let them fade in their own time. I no longer beat up my heart when it fails to deliver the sheer volume of strength that I have become accustomed to expecting from it. I have coaxed my soul to breathe and not be bitter.

To breathe and not be bitter.

The rain is my muse sometimes. It is the sky making love to the earth. The rain is a calm calamity, a release of energy, a signal to sit down and remember to live and love in the moment. It is a flow of nostalgia that drenches your soul.

Rain makes me bloom. The dark clouds hovering in between flickering lightning is a sight that I watch with reverence. I look at the raindrops dancing with the wind and I realise that I am made of the same energy, a minute resemblance of what nature can create, a body encasing the beginning and end of the universe and time.

The rain puts my ego to sleep and brings out the artist in me. I watch the rain and my heart sings melodies from a distant time. We are human. We are here.

We are alive.

she takes broken things
and brings out the beauty in them
like heartbreaking poetry
on discarded paper

if I care, I care with all of me
when you lose me, you lose all of me

there are no leftovers either way

girl,
you are the dark lines of velvet gold
disappearing into the dusk
reappearing again at dawn
you are the fiery splashes of red
generously spilled over the sky
every time you create life
every time you give birth
you are both the beginning
and the finale
you are both pitch black
and blinding white
as well as the rainbow in between
the crescent moon on a cold night
you are both goddess and ghost
the key to all salvation
it is from your heartbeat
that the creation, protection,
and destruction of time unfurls

girl,
you are not a girl
you are a woman
and in the warmth of your belly
sleeps the world

—woman, remember your worth

some days
she is climbing over caverns
tossing hurdles aside
as if her arms were made of steel

some days she is lying
face down on the coarse carpet
of the living room floor
no longer able
to contain all the pain
that she feels

you do not need someone else
to define or rebuild yourself
you do not need a tool
to fix your wounds
you need medicine

you are the medicine

it's all you darling
it was, all along

let go of the *butterflies-in-your-stomach* average love

don't marry them until
you feel *dragons breathing fire*
in your belly
every time you make
eye contact

don't bow down
for just any kind of love
wait for the miracle
wait for the right kind of love

they ask me,
why do I give away pieces
of myself in every person I meet?

they say to me,
why do you always end up
offering so much kindness?
it will kill you one day

but the rain does not fall
where man wills it
it falls in both meadows
and ditches
it cleanses both gardens
and gutters
its purpose is to nourish
the earth
it does not favour
flowers over thorns

it nourishes them all
the dead
the living
and the unborn

I guess you can grow older, but that does not mean you get to forget. I still cry when certain songs play on the radio and I can still remember things that I thought I had buried. It's so cold inside my heart that my blood might as well be a sinister blue from all the frost and dust that has accumulated inside the chambers of my chest.

This is what trauma does.

It's not pretty. It's not something to romanticise and admire. Grief is ugly, hard and foul. There is beauty but there is a lot of stained horror that gets cut off display because people have this twisted notion that any form of tragedy is a trophy, when actually it's a curse. There is healing and growth, but that is only one part of it.

There is so much more that you do not see.

you don't know her

she might seem content
and her mouth might be curved into a dimpled smile.
she might laugh so loud
that music seems like noise next to its sound.
she might make you better
and you might start to believe that she is surely the one.
you might see blotches of bright colour
appearing everywhere in your life
and this might make you feel alive,
make you feel like you love her,
make you feel like you know her.

you don't know her

you see, she is a fixer, a giver.
she is a well of water that never runs out for the needy, but
to reach her core, it's not so easy.
she is a star that guides lost souls back home, but
to reach out and touch her, you need to be something Godly.
she is willing to take away your burdens,
to cure all your ailments and soothe all your burns
but you cannot own the sun without sinking into flames.
she will not be owned.
she will not be tamed.

—how to know her

I want to get out of bed, I really do. But some days this bed is the only place of salvation for this torn soul. The only place where I find no rejection. The only place with open and welcoming arms, though these arms are the seams of my blanket and the warmth is provided by the dull thumping of blood in my anxiously beating heart.

I want to eat healthy, I really do. But some days the comfort of swallowing hot chocolate and tasting the thick, sweet kiss of hazelnut flavoured coffee is the only highlight of my week and I know that most of my money gets wasted on overpriced delicacies that deteriorate any chances of my body being fit, but hey, that's okay. I say that's okay, but is it really okay that I am so hungry for happiness that I am willing to let my body decay?

I want to be happy, I really do. But some days, the cold shouldering of people who just cannot understand my views, who never pay attention to my pain makes me feel lonely and lost and afraid. The years pass by and yet I'm stuck in the past, wishing things would change, but no, they do not change. Sometimes I cry but I feel nothing except numbness, and sometimes I pray but my voice is a whisper and this waiting for a miracle seems pointless and in vain. But still, I pray.

—I want to be honest, I really do

my heart
is a *beast*
it can be wounded
but it cannot be tamed
it can be attacked
but it cannot be controlled

—on wild hearts

with love and kindness
I can be conquered
I can be made
to bend and dance
at your will

but with arrogance and spite
try as you might
I can never be won
I can never be taken
I can never be shaken

you can always start over
you're good at that, remember?

                              —morning mantras

I look like I have it all
but in truth
I am yearning

I look like I'm sunbathing
but in fact
I am burning

—appearances will deceive you

tears are doses of wisdom
drops of pain
drops of medicine
that keep us sane

remember, sweet soul,
the sun should never feel envious
of the sunflower
the source of light
should never feel small

the source of light should never feel small

you think she'll come back every time she leaves
you think she'll come back every time she leaves
you think she'll come back every time she leaves

(she's not coming back this time)

—in case you were still thinking she's coming back

the night is dark and frightening
but that does not mean the sun has died
your patience is what will carry you
safely over to the other side

—the dawn will come in good time

I just want you to know
that you
are unquestionably beautiful
even when you bleed
even when you don't succeed
even when life grips you
tighter around your throat
and you find it hard
to breathe

even then, dearest
you are a work of art

"Why do you run away whenever
someone tries to know you?"

"Because people break things
and I am tired of being broken."

I ask you one thing
and nothing more

do not try to unravel me
if you do not intend
to reach my core

you're an emotional train wreck
and they always get high
over breaking apart
your heart

and you always let them
in the name
of love

I have come to realise that expecting love in return for my love will ultimately destroy me. My love will not always be accepted or appreciated. My kindness will sometimes be ridiculed, even questioned. There will be moments when my affection will be trampled on and my heart will be shoved around like a lost kid in a bustling mob. I will not always be included, remembered, or acknowledged for the person that I am. I may be overlooked and underestimated. My flaws will possibly be enlarged and pointed out in succession. All of my good deeds may entirely be forgotten. My mistakes perhaps magnified on a slide show for all to see. I know that these moments will hurt like hell. They will make me want to howl as they throb in my chest like a raw wound. I can understand pain. I have come to understand that there will always be hurdles and there will always be heavy mornings where the world will seem to be sitting on my heart like a crushing weight. But this time it won't crush me. It won't define my identity.

I won't let it anymore.

love doesn't make you feel afraid
love makes you feel safe
even from yourself
anything less is not love

You delete that song because it reminds you of somebody that you wish you could wipe off the surface of your heart, but you know you can't because their stain is too deep to ever be cleaned out. You take a couple months, maybe even a couple years off to commit to trying new things, failing and trying again, until the memory of them is just an occasional shadow that creeps around you but doesn't damage you anymore. So you discover new songs to love and you listen to them on a high volume in the car with all the windows down because your heart has grown steel wings and you now know that you deserve to be happy and everything is temporary. Your life starts improving, things start changing and the sun is somehow shining brighter than ever before in directions you didn't even know existed. You're too smart to believe in ghosts and goblins, but somehow, on a perfectly good day, you feel like someone (or something) is following you around and the thought unhinges you, but you carry on without complaint. You brush it off as an illusion and you carry on living in your newly found bubble of happiness, but that eerie feeling of being pursued doesn't leave you. It sticks to you. It eats you. Until, one day, you innocently walk into a coffee shop and order that Caribbean mocha that you love, only to lay your eyes on a face sipping coffee or tea or mango juice at a table nearby and your heart nearly explodes in shock, their face a painting of the past you were trying to forget, a stranger perfectly carved so similar to another face you once knew that they could be twins. In that moment, you realise that this is life. This is truth.

Wounds can be sealed. The pain can be masked and sealed.
But scars?

They cannot be erased.

what if I told you
that everything you have seen
and heard
and experienced
is merely a drop
a fraction of a second
a miniature segment
of the journey that
is yet to come?

remember,
sweet soul,
self-destruction
is NEVER
the answer to
sadness

you are not the leaves that
break with the wind

you are the roots
that are strong from within

you carry on
that is your message to the world
you survive, whatever it takes
there are greater things
on their way to you
you need to be ready
when they come

do not allow unworthy and unhealthy energy
to touch your royal soul

What is strength?

Strength is when you choose to forgive
the ones who shattered your heart
instead of choosing to destroy them.

judging the intelligence of a person
based only on their academic performance
instead of their personality
is like finding fault in a fish
for not breathing fire

it's not that she wants to be
alone forever
it's just that she's made the choice
to never settle
until she finds a mind
that understands her
without judgement
and a heart that
feels like
home

—reasons why she's still single

let us not forget the strength
of single mothers
who play two roles
who have endless goals
who have one heart
that beats for two souls

let us celebrate
the single mothers
who are kind
who would move the earth
into a different orbit
if it meant their children
obtained happiness
and peace of mind

let us cherish them
and always remember
that they are magicians
who turn empty rooms
into homes
who turn bread crumbs
into gold

—Happy Father's Day, Mom

she has known tragedy
and it has made her kind

I will either suffocate you
with my over-excessive, eager,
and enveloping love
or
abandon you with my
unforgiving and unalterable indifference

there is absolutely no in-between

you won't understand
until grief pays your heart a visit
you won't understand
until it's the last happy minute
that you can remember
before the darkness came

—they asked me to explain death

you were born into this world
after months of dedication
towards perfecting your creation
every limb of you
is a precisely placed gemstone
every drop of blood in you
is a drop of pure gold
you were perfect
even before you had eyes
so, don't you dare think
for even a moment
that what you see
staring back at you
in the mirror
is flawed

You sit in your towel after a shower, your face the perfect portrait, if sadness had a face. You make coffee with one hand while the other subconsciously wipes away occasional drops of moisture rolling down your cheeks. You make some toasted cheese with a little too much cheese and you watch a TV show you don't like, too busy battling your thoughts to reach out for the remote. You listen to songs that are supposed to make you cry, but you find yourself slow-dancing to them instead. You sing along to familiar random songs on the radio. You sing yourself a lullaby as you settle down in your bed. Your nightmares wake you up in the middle of the night, but you place a hand over your noisy heart, and it calms down instantly.

You smile as you watch the raindrops race each other down the window. You smile and try to get through the day.

You smile and try to get through life this way.

maybe I cannot see
what everyone else can see
because I am too deep in my grief
too busy drowning
to notice the beauty of the waves

you must love yourself, sweet soul
even when you are tired
even when you are angry
even when you are dissatisfied
even when you want to scream so loud
that the heavens shake

you cannot hurt someone
who has absolutely no regard
for your destructive words
who knows the complete power
of their worth
you cannot hurt someone
who is so strong
that nothing can make
their optimism die
your negativity is nothing but
a speck
in their brilliantly blue sky

we all make mistakes
but they are not supposed to make us
or our lives

storms cause ships to sink
but don't determine
that the sun won't rise

I have learned
to treat my
brokenness
as a form of
STRENGTH
instead of
condemning it as a
show of weakness

maybe this life
is simply a memory
and we are all drunk
in a stupor
soon to be awoken by death
to make us sober again

when they pour hate on you
drown them
in your ocean of
deep and engulfing kindness

your inability to see my worth
does not, even in the slightest way,
make me unworthy
of giving
and receiving
love

no matter how much you love someone
you cannot be their lifeboat and save them
if you are sinking in the deep end yourself

healing has to start with you first

you can't make them see
who you really are
they don't really have a clue

the trick is, darling
it doesn't matter if they don't
as long as you do

you fade away
the minute I let you peep into
my soul

the light inside must have blinded your eyes

losing a coward
doesn't make me less whole
I have seen too many to be afraid of goodbyes

What is love?

Love is wiping the sweat from her face after you both finished moving furniture together. Love is wiping the tears from her face after a heated shouting match. Love is making coffee for her in the morning before she wakes up and secretly taking a photo of her sipping it with wild hair and sleepy eyes. Love is buying the handbag she's been stealing glances at in the shop window for months and surprising her with it on a Sunday. Love is making fun of her singing and smearing tomato sauce all over her nose, then running away laughing as she starts chasing you. Love is packing an extra sanitary pad in her handbag and checking she has her keys, because you know she has a habit of forgetting essential things. Love is playing with her hair and calling her crazy, but with a smile on your face because her crazy is exactly the kind of crazy you need in your life. Love is watching her sleep, and praying to God that she never has a night of troubled sleep in her life.

How do you know this?

By watching my parents never stop falling in love with each other, over and over again.

this pain will temporarily cripple you
but it won't crush you

my grief is shed
along these trails on my cheeks
these damp tear stains

peacefully, patiently, perfectly

like petals drifting off a rose
like drops of moisture signalling rain
conveying nothing but harmony
concealing all signs of pain

this is my face
merely a surface
of the soul
that inhabits
this shell

this is simply
just shallow waters
you haven't met
my storms

this is my stillness
my serene state
of calm

you do not know
how it feels
to submerge
in my calamity
to surrender to my chaos

you cannot scratch
this surface
and call it science
I am beyond
what the eye
can see

—in honour of every woman

haven't you seen her sparkle?
she made the stars stand in line

why do you hold back from
giving yourself
that unconditional kindness
that you never hesitate to shower on
everybody else?

you are not
the snowflake

you are the storm

I'm sensitive. It's not something that I try to hide.
I'm not at all ashamed of my oversized love.
I give my all to everything and sometimes,
it leaves me destroyed.
I love greatly,
and as a result, *I suffer greatly.*

I am not less because I do not have your love
I am not less because you decided I am less
than worthy of your kindness
I am not less because you decided to break me
then proceed to blame me
for these injuries
that I did not want for me
I am not less because you have it all and I
have nothing but this breath
this life that heaves in my chest
I am not less because you have a heart so cold
that you itch to extinguish anything that
threatens your icy ego
I am not less because you are a cannibal
feasting on the hearts and souls
of those who trusted you
more than they trusted the Lord

I am not less
I am not less
I am not less

on the contrary
I am a woman

and I am not less
I am more
than anything you have ever imagined
than anything you can ever be

I see forever in places
where temporary is triumphant
and slammed doors are
the only thing written in stone

my dear
you are the whole sun

don't let your dark spots
or your stretch marks
or your bruised heart
make you forget
that without you
there would be
no life on earth

she's a shell now
once a treasure chest
once a safe-keeper
of priceless gold
she's a shadow of a soul
now sold
she's a memory of a warm heart
now cold

—on shadows

this is a society
that will try
and fail
to break your wings
and then
complain so righteously
about your wings being made
of steel
and how wrong that is

Indifference
has DESTROYED
more hearts
than
hate
ever will.

if you let yourself fall in love
with only appearances
again and again
then you can't deny
that you deserve
to be deceived

It was not the possibility of pain that frightened her. She has been in the very centre of endless chaos all her life. No, it was the possibility that she may end up enduring all that pain for the wrong person that terrified her. It was the thought of becoming caught in a cycle of doubt and inevitably wasting her kindness over a smile that made her quiver in fear.

—on doubtful love

may your heart never falter
in its speed

for I know you are stronger than you seem

it's too dark and cold in this world
to keep drenching those whom we love
with icy words

speak love
breathe kindness
live with compassion

be the fire that guides a lost soul home

It was an eternity all in a second. A sliver of a weakness. For a minute, all was forgotten. She needed water and the rains were late this year. The future appeared bleak. The present was deceiving, stealing away her dreams. The past was lost, and her thoughts were scattered. She was hurt, and she needed a rag to tie her wounds tight. So she forgot that she cannot reach for what she has already forsaken. What she really needed was a light and it didn't matter from where it came. So she burned it all. Her heart. Her flaws. Her pain. Her fears.

The pile of ashes that remained were bathed in her tears.

she was starving so badly
craving for the most delicious things

not for her stomach, but for her soul

I keep giving and giving away
pieces of my soul
so terribly generously
even after everything
is taken from me
that is my tragedy

—on loss of self

your heart is a war zone
and this life
is just raining bullets

it's a thin line
between what is real
and what is not
apple juice looks like liquor
sugar looks like salt
we believe things are sweet
only to find out they are bitter
this heart is weak and fickle
all this pain is sometimes
its own fault

I wish I could say
that loving me
is easy

but it is not

loving me is like
loving the ocean
some days, the waves are cool
and graceful
caressing your tired feet
with such patience and love

but some days
the waves are rough
unforgiving
and cold
ready to pull you in
and sink you to the bottom
if you don't know
how to swim

you need people who will
stick around longer
who will stay behind
without question
to clean up the damage
and pick up the pieces

you need people who will
pull you out from under the ashes
not like ancient bone dust
from a decayed corpse
but like the roaring birth
of a phoenix

—on friendship

may you never be afraid
to listen to the songs of your heart
and may you always have the courage
to loudly sing along

they ask me why I am still single
unmarried
not committed
not looking for a husband
like my life depends on it

they look at me and
they say,
you are a pretty girl
who would do well
as a wife
but you are almost reaching
your mid-twenties
your youth is decaying

they stare at me curiously
at weddings
at birthdays
at funerals
and they ask me,
who will you spend this life
and all its milestones with?
woman! don't you see?
without a man, you are incomplete!

so I look back at them
and I say,

a man is not a crutch
a woman is not a machine
and if a life of love
is not in the picture
then being single is the
greatest blessing
I have ever received

—love (for) marriage

she is not easy
she is not the girl
who walks the path that
the majority of people take

she stands out

her heart is big
and her dreams are loud
you can't become a part
of her world
without opening your wings
and leaving the ground

she is a galaxy in motion

she has no time
for simple clouds

the moment you feel like
evil has won
life is a blank void
and all hope is lost
that is the moment
miracles start
to manifest
that is the moment
the universe itself
will intervene
to save you

—reasons to keep breathing

looking at stars
always leaves me in awe
here I stand, a minute particle
observing glowing gods
that blink at me
from billions of miles away
and yet, my bones
are made from the same silver light
that is emitted by every twinkling inhabitant
of the glorious night sky

she still spills kindness
even after being drenched
in disappointment
by people who cannot distinguish
the difference
between a rock
and a gem

I am far from perfect.

Usually, I am a concoction of insecurities and confusions and catastrophes all wrapped nicely with a bright pink ribbon on top. If you know me, you will know that I detest pink. I am angry, adorable, easily annoyed. I am also taken advantage of. You cannot break me, but I promise that you can bend me around to the satisfaction of your will. Internally, I am unhappy consistently, only joyful occasionally. Externally, you will never have a clue of what is happening in this soul. I am a bit of an insomniac, and anxiety has been a dominating presence in my life, especially in the last few years. I seem content, but there's utter chaos underneath that carefully mastered calm that you see on the surface. I am not easily understandable, and I like it that way. I am not afraid of pain or death.

I am afraid of dying while still alive, my soul going dry, my lost thoughts churning as a black hole sucks me away, yet every limb in my body still functioning.

Every bone in my body *still burning*.

I have a tired heart
that never gets tired of
reaching out to help people
who are too tired to reach out
and save it when it falls

flowers
and music
and winter blues

everywhere I go
I can't help but
leave little clues

—three things that I love

you care for things
that neglect you
and die for things
that reject you

—reasons why it hurts

It comes like a clawed hand that wraps its talons around your throat in the middle of the night. A quiet black cloud that seems like a tiny dot in the distant sky, but suddenly it's so close that it's floating inches above your head. You think your heart is safe, but in the early hours of the dawn it's back to leaking again, the loud dripping of confusion, pain, and desperation from its seams serving as a reminder that you are not as content and fine and okay as you had thought you were. Your eyes are welling over, and before you reach out to catch it, the tear drops grace the floor. You try to make sense of everything, but nothing comes as a solution. Nothing comes as an answer. There's just this restless fluttering in your chest like your heart has wings and wants to be released from its rib cage. You don't know how to release it. You don't know how to silence it. So you just suffer. Until it stops.

Until it becomes still again.

—*the meaning of anxiety*

there are days when
my existence is brimming with
thick, sweet emotion
you can almost see
the flood of honey
being contained by
this brittle body

but there are also days
when my bones become
hollow, cold
breathing is a burden
this body is still alive
but it is empty
my blood is black
my voice an echo

—episodes

every time you refuse to allow
the lies, deceit, and negative energy of others
to disrupt your inner peace
you win

—keep winning

judging the intelligence
of a person
based only on
their academic performance
instead of their personality
is like finding fault in
a fish
for not breathing fire

You will only understand what damage to the soul feels like when you finish a phone call that felt like Satan just told you he was on his way to your door with an army of demons. Then, two days later, you're cramped in the back of a packed SUV that's speeding towards a city that you don't want to go to, because you know that what's awaiting you at the end of the road was far worse than being led by the devil to Hell's gates. You'd rather bury yourself alive than show up at that funeral, and yet you still show up anyway. You wish it was you in that casket. You wish you could take the last two days back. To change things. To change everything.

To stop death in its tracks, instead of having reality painfully point out the facts.

WITHERED roses
remind me that
there is still
beauty
left to BE
SEEN
in wrecked things

~~tragedy~~ courage was her middle name

this heart is not a place
to park your sorrows
nor a playground
where you can stomp
on blades of grass
to get rid of the
bitter taste
of your past

you think a good woman
is a playground
you drink her love
like wine
and you discard her emotions
like debris in the wind
you think you are entitled
to have her
in your life
in your heart
in your world
well, let me tell you this

she is a privilege
never an entitlement
she is a blessing
never a burden

a good woman is
the face of divinity
prosperity
purity
never a liability

you promise her respect
and attention
but all she's seen so far
is contempt
and alienation
so how do you expect her
to stick around?

stars weren't made to linger on the ground

you think that
by somehow breaking
everything
and everyone around you
it will help you feel
less broken
but it won't
because haven't you heard?
acid cannot nurse
a wilted tree back to life
only rain can do that
and everything else
is self-destruction

puddles are common,
shallow

she wasn't looking for
another pothole
full of muddy rainwater

she was looking for the ocean

It's really a bit sad, isn't it?

What is sad?

That you are always the fireplace where people huddle next to when it snows, but they never realise all the soot and smoke that you handle just to give them warmth. They never realise the cold existence you suffer when it's lonely in the summer.

It's easy to love the light. The soft, tender smiles. The happy, carefree face that wants to pull you closer and laugh in the middle of a pillow fight. It's effortless to love a sunny sky, a perfect rose, a cool breeze in the middle of summer.

But that's not the love you really need.

When winter comes, and your heart turns to stone cold, will they light a torch to melt your pain? When the winds howl and the rains pour down like the sky has flooded, will they build a raft to hold you afloat? When you are no longer the angel they have known but the demon of the darkness that they fear, will they stay despite every cell in their body wailing for them to flee? When loving you is hard, when the pillow fights become wars and bloodshed is involved, will they still hold on? When you can't look at your own face without loathing it, will they show you the love that once gave you the strength to love your own imperfections? Oh, it's easy to love candlelight and its kind warmth.

It's hard to love fire when you're burning in hell.

don't spill mud
on a person's heart
and accuse them of being
unclean

an old photo
in a new photo frame
chilli flakes
inside a chocolate cake
she was a woman
that you could never really explain
she was a changing horizon
in a sky that remained
forever the same

—you're unlucky if you lose her

My writing has always been my haven. Home. The place where my heart rests and roars at the same time. It is how I teach myself to breathe again when the air feels thick and my lungs feel heavy from all my worries. It's my outlet for everything. I take my pain and pour it out unfiltered through my poetry. I use ink to ease my throbbing wounds. I write because I have never known how else to express who I really am. Writing is how I show the world that I am alive. That I am here and that I have a heartbeat.

Writing is how I know I am worthy.

This is my art.

thank you

A book is not something that can be created overnight. It is the labour of not only the author but a team of magicians who turn my ideas into reality and my thoughts into achievements. I am indebted to my wonderful team at Thought Catalog who took my raw words and helped me create this beautiful collection of poetry. I have no words to truly explain how grateful I am that you exist. Special thanks to Marisa Donnelly, my producer and Alex Zulauf, my book producer, who have been immensely supportive of my writing from the very beginning and continue to inspire me with their kindness. I am also grateful to my beautiful mom and little sister for being with me through everything and for giving me unconditional love throughout my journey. I am blessed beyond measure to have you. Thank you for your love. It has given me strength.

My dear readers, I would like to extend my heartfelt love and gratitude to you. Thank you for giving me your heart as I have given you mine. I wish you the purest form of healing. I wish you joy. Most of all, I wish you love and the abundance of it in every day of your lives.

about the author

Abirami P. Kurukkal is a writer and visual artist studying Psychology in South Africa. Rudra is her second book of poetry. Abirami has been writing all her life and has had a profound love for English, literature, writing and poetry since her childhood. She hopes to encourage positive change in communities, and eradicate the stigma surrounding various social issues, through her self-expression.

YOU MIGHT ALSO LIKE:

Remember Me as a Time of Day by Abirami P. Kurukkal

Salt Water by Brianna Wiest

We Are All Just A Collection Of Cords by Chrissy Stockton

THOUGHT
CATALOG
Books

THOUGHT
CATALOG
Books

Thought Catalog Books is a publishing house owned by The
Thought & Expression Company, an independent media
group based in Brooklyn, NY. Founded in 2010, we are com-
mitted to facilitating thought and expression. We exist to
help people become better communicators and listeners in
order to engender a more exciting, attentive, and imaginative
world.

Visit us on the web at
www.thoughtcatalogbooks.com and *www.collective.world.*

www.ingramcontent.com/pod-product-compliance
Lightning Source LLC
LaVergne TN
LVHW041315080426
835513LV00008B/477